Pet Care

Mice

Rebecca Sjonger & Bobbie Kalman

Photographs by Marc Crabtree

Crabtree Publishing Company

www.crabtreebooks.com

Mice

A Bobbie Kalman Book

Dedicated by Rebecca Sjonger
To the Lunch Table—you asked for it!

Editor-in-Chief
Bobbie Kalman

Writing team
Rebecca Sjonger
Bobbie Kalman

Substantive editor
Kathryn Smithyman

Editors
Amanda Bishop
Kelley MacAulay

Art director
Robert MacGregor

Design
Margaret Amy Reiach

Production coordinator
Heather Fitzpatrick

Photo research
Crystal Foxton
Kristina Lundblad

Consultant
Dr. Michael A. Dutton, DVM, DABVP
Exotic and Bird Clinic of New Hampshire
www.exoticandbirdclinic.com

Special thanks to
Devan Cruickshanks, Brody Cruickshanks, Heather
and Tim Cruickshanks, Steve Cruickshanks, Kyle Foxton,
Doug Foxton, Aimee Lefebvre, Alissa Lefebvre, Jacquie Lefebvre,
Jeremy Payne, Dave Payne, Kathy Middleton, Natasha Barrett,
Mike Cipryk and PETLAND

Photographs
Ian Beames/ardea.com: page 10
Marc Crabtree: front cover, title page, pages, 5, 6, 11, 13,
    14 (except mouse), 15, 16-17, 18 (bottom), 19 (top), 21 (top),
    22, 23, 24, 25, 28, 30, 31
© Dwight R. Kuhn: pages 3, 7, 12
Robert MacGregor: page 21 (bottom)
PhotoDisc: page 4
Other images by Comstock and PhotoDisc

Illustrations
All illustrations by Margaret Amy Reiach

Digital prepress
Embassy Graphics

Printer
Worzalla Publishing Company

Crabtree Publishing Company

www.crabtreebooks.com   1-800-387-7650

PMB 16A	612 Welland Avenue	73 Lime Walk
350 Fifth Avenue	St. Catharines	Headington
Suite 3308	Ontario	Oxford
New York, NY	Canada	OX3 7AD
10118	L2M 5V6	United Kingdom

Cataloging-in-Publication Data
Sjonger, Rebecca.
  Mice / Rebecca Sjonger & Bobbie Kalman;
photographs by Marc Crabtree.
    p. cm. -- (Pet care series)
  Includes index.
   ISBN 0-7787-1754-2 (RLB) -- ISBN 0-7787-1786-0 (pbk.)
  1. Mice as pets--Juvenile literature. [1. Mice as pets. 2. Pets.]
I. Kalman, Bobbie. II. Crabtree, Marc, ill. III. Title. IV. Series.
SF459.M5S56 2004
636.935'3--dc22
                                                            2003027238
                                                            LC

Contents

What are mice?

Mice are **mammals**. Mammals have fur or hair on their bodies. They also have backbones. Mother mammals make milk inside their bodies to feed their babies. Mice are part of a group of mammals called **rodents**. Most rodents have small bodies and sharp front teeth.

A mouse's body

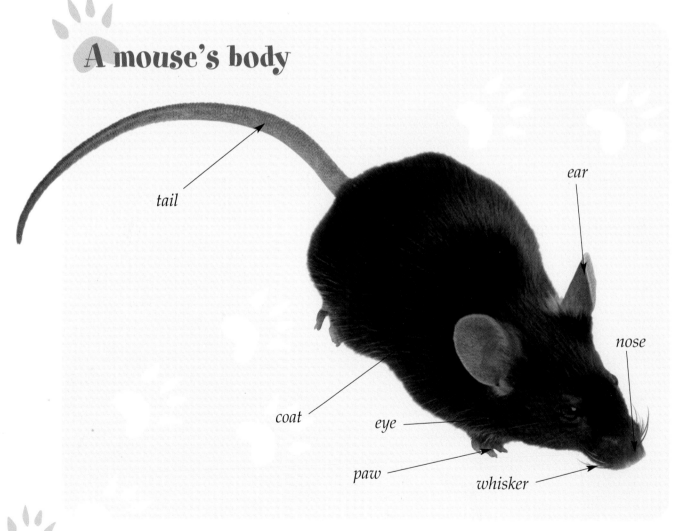

tail

coat

eye

paw

ear

nose

whisker

Mouse history

Thousands of years ago, all mice were **wild**, or not tame. Some wild mice snuck into people's warm homes and nibbled on their food! People began catching these wild mice and keeping them as pets. Mice are now a popular pet all around the world. Like wild mice, most pet mice sleep all day long. They wake up to eat and play in the evening.

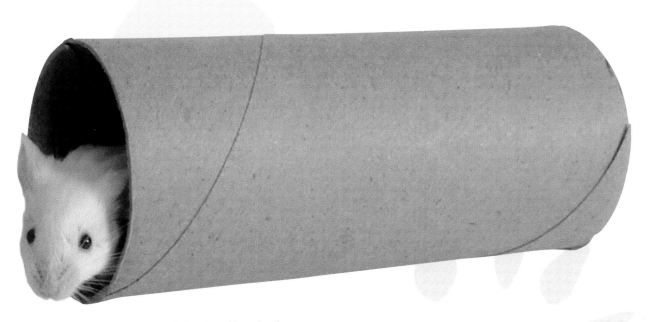

*Wild mice live in **burrows**, or underground tunnels. Pet mice may use cardboard tubes as burrows!*

The right pet for you?

Did you know that mice are very loving animals? They like living and playing with other mice. They even like to be around people! Mice are also very curious. They will explore their cages and watch everything that goes on around them. As well as playing with and loving your pet mouse, you will have to feed it, clean its cage, and help it stay healthy.

If you put something new in front of a mouse, it will want to check it out!

Are you ready?

The questions below will help you and your family decide if you are ready for a pet mouse.

- Do you have other pets that may scare or hurt a mouse?

- Is there a quiet space in your home where you can put a cage?

- Will you clean out the whole cage at least once a week?

- Who will feed the mouse and give it fresh water every day?

- Do you have time to play with a mouse every evening?

- Is anyone in your family **allergic** to mice? Mouse allergies can be very dangerous!

Many mice!

There are over 1,000 **species**, or kinds, of mice. Almost all mice that are kept as pets are part of a species called **house mice**. Some people keep other species as pets, but they are much less common. These unusual mice include zebra mice, pygmy mice, and Egyptian spiny mice. Find out more about them on these pages!

Popular pets

Your pet mouse will most likely be a tamed house mouse. At first, all house mice had coats that were shades of brown and gray. Over time, **albino**, or pure white, coats became very common. When mice with different types of coats **mated**, baby mice were born with coats of many colors, patterns, and fur lengths.

Most pet mice are around six inches (15 cm) long from their heads to the tips of their tails.

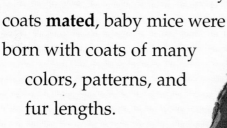

Zebra mice have golden brown coats with dark brown stripes. They are around eight inches (20 cm) long from head to tail.

Pygmy mice are one of the smallest mammals! They are less than four inches (10 cm) long from head to tail.

Egyptian spiny mice have spiky-looking coats. They are around twelve inches (30.5 cm) from head to tail.

Baby mice

Baby mice are called **pinkies**. They are born in **litters**, or groups, of up to sixteen mice. When pinkies are born, they have no fur. They cannot see or hear. Their mother protects and feeds them.

A mother mouse feeds her pinkies milk from her body.

All grown up

Most pinkies start growing fur on their bodies after three days. After ten days, they can see and hear. When pinkies are three weeks old, they need more than their mother's milk to eat. They become adult mice when they are just twelve weeks old! At that age, they can have their own baby mice.

Keep adult female and male mice apart so they cannot mate.

No unwanted mice!

Mother mice can have baby mice around eight times a year. If you let your mouse mate and have pinkies, they will start to add up! If your mouse does have babies, make sure you find good homes for all of them before they grow up.

Picking your mouse

To find a pet mouse, check your local **animal shelter**, or ask friends and family if they know of any mice that are being given away. You can also buy your mouse from a pet store or a **breeder**. Make sure that you get your pet from people who take very good care of their animals.

Friends forever

Most mice enjoy the company of other mice. Mice from the same litter will likely get along well. Choose two or more mice that are the same sex to avoid unwanted baby mice. If you get only one mouse, you will need to give it a lot of love to keep it from being lonely.

What to look for

Take your time when you are picking the mouse you want as your pet. You will probably want the most playful one. Make sure it is also healthy! Ways to tell if it is healthy are listed below.

- active, curious behavior
- a sleek, strong body
- shiny, thick fur
- bright, clean eyes
- a clean nose and bottom and clean ears
- no bites, sores, or bald spots on its body
- other healthy mice living with it in its cage

13

Getting ready

Before you bring your mouse home, get everything you need ready for your new pet. Some of the things that you will need to care for your mouse are shown on these pages.

If you are getting two or more mice, buy a big cage that has plenty of room for both.

*Buy a bag of **bedding**, such as aspen shavings, for the bottom of the cage.*

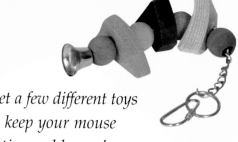

Get a few different toys to keep your mouse active and happy!

A small house or box will give your mouse a dark, quiet place to hide away when it is sleeping.

Buy a **ceramic** food bowl. Your mouse will not be able to tip it over or gnaw holes in it!

A **salt lick** helps your mouse get the salt it needs in its diet.

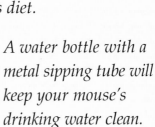

A water bottle with a metal sipping tube will keep your mouse's drinking water clean.

Give your mouse fruit-tree branches to gnaw on and keep its teeth healthy.

Get both fresh and packaged foods to keep your mouse healthy.

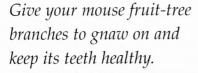

Welcome home!

When you pick up your new mouse, take along a carrying cage or a small cardboard box with air holes in it. Your pet can travel safely in the cage. Visit a **veterinarian** or "vet" on your way home. The vet will check your mouse to make sure it is healthy. At home, give your mouse time to get used to you and your family.

Mouse house

You can get a good cage for your mouse at a pet store. Make sure plenty of fresh air can get into the cage. Most cages have plastic bases and wire mesh tops. Make sure the wires go all the way to the bottom of the cage, or your mouse may escape by chewing through the plastic! Small mice and pinkies may even be able to slip through the wires. The spaces between the wires need to be much smaller than your mouse's body is!

Different levels give your mouse more room to play.

Cleaning the cage often will help keep it from smelling bad.

16

Putting the water bottle outside the cage saves space inside for your mouse.

Some of the things to look for when picking the best spot to put the cage are listed below.

 quiet so your mouse can sleep during the day

 not too sunny

 between 65°F and 80°F (18°C to 26°C)

 not overly **humid**

Cover the floor of the cage with at least one inch (2.5 cm) of bedding. Avoid cedar and pine shavings—these woods could make your pet very sick!

Meals for mice

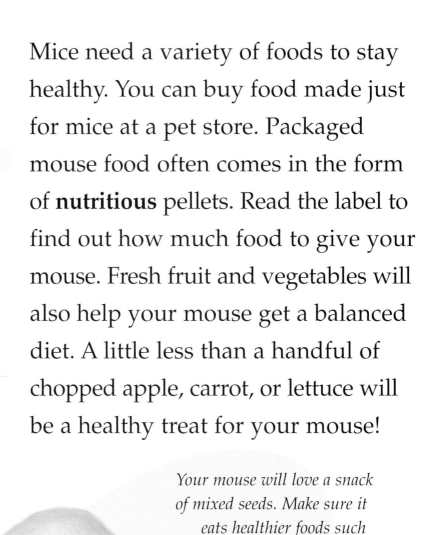

Mice need a variety of foods to stay healthy. You can buy food made just for mice at a pet store. Packaged mouse food often comes in the form of **nutritious** pellets. Read the label to find out how much food to give your mouse. Fresh fruit and vegetables will also help your mouse get a balanced diet. A little less than a handful of chopped apple, carrot, or lettuce will be a healthy treat for your mouse!

Your mouse will love a snack of mixed seeds. Make sure it eats healthier foods such as pellets as well!

18

Fresh water

Drinking fresh water will help keep your mouse healthy. Make sure the bottle is always full of clean water. Watch out for leaky bottles! Thoroughly wash and rinse the water bottle every day.

Not on the menu

Be very careful when you choose which food to give your mouse. Some foods can make your pet very ill!

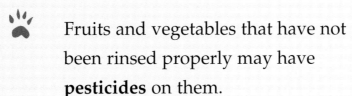

Fruits and vegetables that have not been rinsed properly may have **pesticides** on them.

Never offer your mouse raw meat, which can make it very sick.

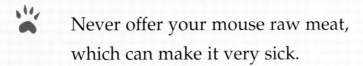

Never give your mouse rotten food. Make sure to take old food out of the cage every day.

Candy and treats such as chocolate are not healthy for your mouse.

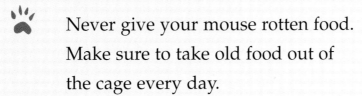

Mouse grooming

Most mice are clean animals. They spend a lot of time **grooming**, or cleaning, their bodies. Your mouse uses its paws and teeth to keep its coat clean and looking good. Digging and gnawing help it keep its teeth and claws short. Your pet may need your help with grooming, though.

Your mouse will be happy if it can keep itself clean!

Trim teeth

Mice have four **incisors**, or sharp front teeth, which never stop growing. Gnawing helps grind down a mouse's teeth and keep them from getting too long. Your mouse will gnaw on just about anything! A great healthy item for gnawing is a piece of fruit-tree wood.

Keep them short!

Your mouse's claws may grow too long if it does not have wood or cardboard to scratch. If its claws grow so long that they begin to curl, ask your vet to show you how to trim them. You must be very careful when you cut the claws yourself, because they may bleed if they are cut too short.

Always use scissors or clippers that are made just for trimming rodent claws.

Handle with care

Give your mouse at least one day to explore its cage and begin to feel at home. You can then train it to be **handled**, or picked up. Always wash your hands before handling your mouse. Follow the steps on these pages to help your pet become used to being picked up.

Let your mouse crawl from hand to hand so it can keep moving around.

Hand training

Your mouse needs to become used to your smell. Let it sniff your fingers and hands. You can hold out a few seeds to get your mouse interested. Do not offer food every time, though, or your pet will always want a treat!

Use both hands when you pick up your mouse. Never hold a mouse by its tail, which can snap right off!

Handy mice

When your mouse is used to your smell, it may climb onto your palm. Keep your hand close to the floor or near a tabletop, so if your mouse falls or jumps, it will not get hurt. You can now try picking up the mouse.

Play time!

Mice are very active at night. They love jumping, climbing, digging, hiding, and running. Make sure there are enough things for your mouse to do in its cage. Playing gives it a lot of exercise and keeps it healthy. These pages show some common mouse toys that will keep your pet active and happy.

Dangling toys can be hung from the top of the cage.

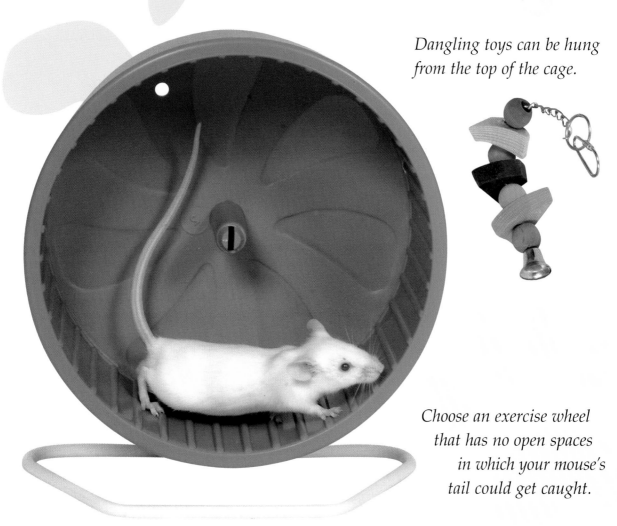

Choose an exercise wheel that has no open spaces in which your mouse's tail could get caught.

24

One change at a time

Keep the cage interesting for your mouse. Try adding new toys or moving toys from one area of the cage to another area. Take your time making changes, though. If you switch more than one thing at a time, your mouse may become confused.

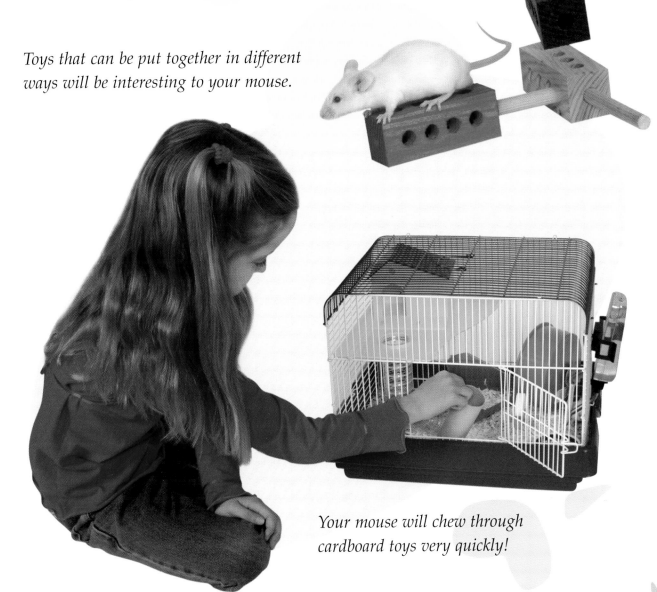

Toys that can be put together in different ways will be interesting to your mouse.

Your mouse will chew through cardboard toys very quickly!

Mouse messages

Did you know that your mouse can send you messages? Watch how it moves its body, ears, and tail. Listen for the sounds it makes. Your mouse may be trying to tell you something important! Some common ways that mice express themselves are shown on these pages.

A happy mouse has a relaxed body, a still tail, and its ears pointed forward.

*A mouse that is angry flattens its ears against its head, **vibrates** its tail, and has a stiff body.*

A curious mouse rises up on its back legs. It may also look around or sniff the air.

Happy mice groom themselves. If your mouse is grooming itself all the time or very roughly, however, it is telling you that it is nervous.

Squeak!

Mice "speak" to one another by squeaking. They are so quiet, though, that you might not be able to hear them! Their squeaks may become louder when they are fighting.

Staying safe

Your mouse will not bite you unless you startle it. You can avoid being bitten by leaving your mouse alone when it is sleeping. Remember to be gentle and careful when you are handling your pet. Never startle it when you pick it up! If you are bitten by your mouse, try not to drop or squeeze it.

Show your family and friends how to handle your mouse properly.

Outdoor dangers

You may think that it is natural to let your mouse play outdoors. There are many dangers outdoors, though. Cats or birds may see your mouse as a tasty treat! Never allow your mouse to roam around outdoors. It may become scared and run away.

Look out!

Before you let your mouse out of its cage, look for these possible dangers.

- Are there doors or windows that your mouse can use to escape?

- Is there any furniture or an area in which your mouse may hide?

- Is there anything in the room that your mouse may damage with its teeth or claws?

- Are there **poisonous** plants that your mouse can reach and eat?

- Are there exposed electrical cords that may harm your mouse if it bites them?

Your pet cat may be the greatest danger to your mouse!

Visiting a vet

A veterinarian is a medical doctor who treats animals. He or she will help you keep your mouse healthy. If you think your mouse may be sick, take it to see a vet right away. The sooner your mouse is treated by a vet, the better are its chances of surviving an illness!

If you ever have any questions about your mouse's health, your vet can help you.

When to get help

It is very important to take your mouse to a vet at the first sign of an illness. Watch for any of the warning signs listed below.

 sleeping more than usual

 wheezing, trouble breathing, or sneezing

 runny eyes or nose

sores or scabs appearing on its skin

losing fur

 a wet bottom

A wonderful life

You need to treat your mouse with great care. Proper feeding, grooming, and handling will make it very happy and healthy. A healthy pet mouse will live for one to three years. Have fun playing and caring for your pet, and it will have a great life with you!

Words to know

Note: Boldfaced words that are defined in the book may not appear on this page.

allergic Describing someone who has a physical reaction to something such as a food or animal dander

animal shelter A center that cares for animals that do not have owners

breeder A person who brings mice together so the mice can make babies

ceramic Describing something that is made out of baked clay

humid Describing air that contains water vapor, which makes the air damp or moist

mate To join together to make babies

nutritious Describing food that contains materials needed by a body to grow and stay healthy

pesticide Chemical made to kill insects

poisonous Describing something that has substances in it that may harm or kill an animal

veterinarian A medical doctor who treats animals

vibrate To move rapidly back and forth or up and down

wheeze To breathe with difficulty, usually with a whistling sound

Index

1 2 3 4 5 6 7 8 9 0   Printed in the U.S.A.   3 2 1 0 9 8 7 6 5 4